IMAGES
of America

MORRISTOWN

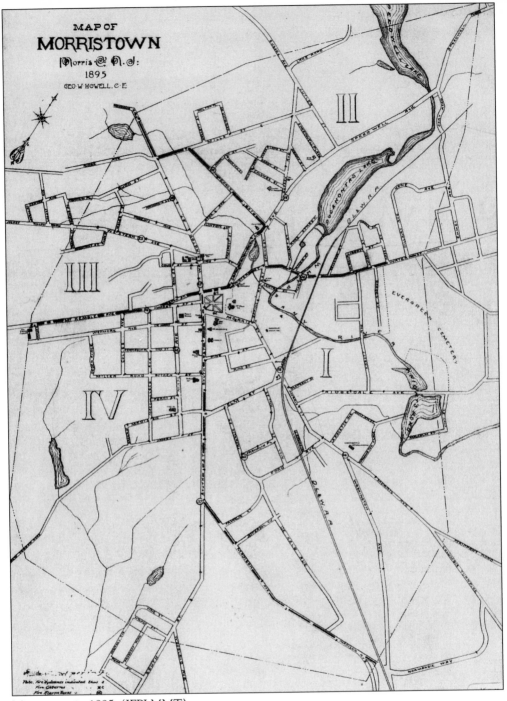

Morristown in 1895. (JFPLMMT)

IMAGES
of America

MORRISTOWN

Joan M. Williams

ARCADIA

ISBN 0-7524-0207-2

Published by Arcadia Publishing,
an imprint of the Chalford Publishing Corporation
One Washington Center, Dover, New Hampshire 03820
Printed in Great Britain

Library of Congress Cataloging-in-Publication Data applied for

A *c.* 1850 oil painting of Morristown by Charles J. Ogden. (JFPLMMT)

Contents

Acknowledgments

My thanks go to all who contributed to this book—individuals, historical societies, libraries—who trusted me with their irreplaceable and treasured photographs and mementos.

To Archie Beiser, Jean and Homer Hill, June Kennedy, the Historical Society of Somerset Hills (HSSH), and the Bernardsville Library Local History Room: thank you.

Also, I wish to thank Sarah Henrich of Historic Speedwell; Leslie Douthwaite and the staff of the Local History and Genealogy Department at the Joint Free Public Library of Morristown and Morris Township (JFPLMMT); Alice Caulkins and Jane Odenweller at the Macculloch Hall Historical Museum (MHHM); Jeanne H. Watson, Director of the Morris County Historical Society at Acorn Hall (MCHS); Alan Stein, Archivist of the National Park Service at Washington's Headquarters; and Samuel S. Singleton Jr., Executive Director, and Marge Morreale, Assistant Director, of Neighborhood House. And I cannot neglect to thank Beth, Dawn, and Erin at the Budget Print Center.

This book would not have been possible without all of you. Thank you!

References

Acorn Hall. 1980. Morristown, New Jersey: Morris County Historical Society.

Cavanaugh, Cam. 1994. *In Lights and Shadows*. Morristown, New Jersey: The Joint Free Public Library of Morristown and Morris Township.

Cavanaugh, Cam, Barbara Hoskins, and Frances D. Pingeon. 1981. *At Speedwell in the Nineteenth Century*. Morristown, New Jersey: The Speedwell Village.

Foy, Sally Fairchild, and Linda Z. Winterberg. 1980. *Macculloch Hall . . . A Family Album*. Morristown, New Jersey: The Junior League of Morristown, Inc.

Introduction

Although "Morristown" evokes pictures of ragged troops huddled in log huts, shivering in the bitter cold of winter, there is more to the town than the Revolutionary War.

By the time Washington's soldiers were encamped in Jockey Hollow, the village of Morristown was at the hub of roads leading out in all directions. Settled in the early eighteenth century, Morristown became the seat of Morris County, which had been set off from Hunterdon County in 1739.

Morristown residents numbered close to 250 in the middle of the eighteenth century. Local newspapers reported items such as rewards for the capture and return for runaway slaves, accidents—often involving horses, sales of property, deaths, and a stage wagon to what is now Jersey City.

At the time of the Revolution the village of Morristown had the services of two churches, a court house, two taverns, two schoolhouses, and several stores, as well as access to mills and iron forges in the surrounding area.

Washington twice made his winter headquarters in Morristown. In 1778–79 he stayed in Arnold's Tavern while his troops were billeted in local houses, barns, and fields. During that terrible and infamous winter of 1779–80, Washington lived in the Ford Mansion, home of Jacob Ford, while his troops camped in Jockey Hollow. It was there that Tempe Wick became famous when she hid her horse in her bedroom to save it from scavenging soldiers. That winter also saw Alexander Hamilton courting—and winning—Elizabeth (Betsy) Schuyler at the home of Dr. Jabez Campfield. The couple were married in the same house, now known as the Schuyler-Hamilton House and owned by the Daughters of the American Revolution as their headquarters and museum.

Major General Benedict Arnold, who was never brought to trial for his treasonous actions, was court-martialled in Dickerson Tavern for lesser offenses; he was found guilty (and publically reprimanded) of allowing an enemy vessel into port without official approval, and using official wagons to transport private property.

The Marquis de Lafayette payed an overnight visit to Morristown in July 1825, and was ceremoniously welcomed and dined.

By the beginning of the nineteenth century Morristown was a thriving community: the Morris Academy, a preparatory school, was educating boys and girls; the library had opened in 1792 with ninety-six volumes; and Stephen Vail was operating the Speedwell Iron Works. It was there that Stephen's son, Alfred, helped Samuel F.B. Morse perfect the telegraph, and where, on January 6, 1838, the electromagnetic telegraph was first demonstrated.

There was a Fire Association serving the area and a new court house was built on Washington Street. The Morris Canal, brainchild of George Macculloch, opened in 1831 and the first railroad chugged into town on New Year's Day, 1838. On April 6, 1865, Morristown was incorporated by the New Jersey State Legislature.

Morristown began to attract wealthy New Yorkers who built mansions, many of which can still be seen in the area of Macculloch and Maple Avenues. Thomas Nast, the "father of the political cartoon" and famous for his Santa Claus, Tammany Tiger, and Uncle Sam depictions, came to town in 1870.

For entertainment, people indulged in sports such as tennis, golf, bicycling, polo, and hunting. Less strenuous activities included reading clubs, cooking classes, parties, games, and amateur dramatics, the latter often as benefits.

The 50,000-volume Library and Lyceum, opened in 1878, housed a public reading room, the Morris Academy, an audience hall with stage and boxes, and a ballroom with dressing and retiring rooms. After the building burned in 1914, a new library was opened in 1917 at its present location on Miller Road.

The Association of Work Among the Italians opened in 1898, instructing the new immigrants in English and providing services for their children. As the ethnic population of Morristown changed and made use of the Association, it was renamed Neighborhood House in 1912.

The twentieth century saw many changes in Morristown. The first trolley rumbled around the Green in 1909, and motor cars soon appeared on the streets. Young men and women went off to serve, and many to die for, their country in the two World Wars.

Buildings were added and improved around the Green and, in the 1960s, urban renewal began as old buildings were removed to make way for the present-day Headquarters Plaza. Corporations have taken the place of many of the large mansions, new highways have been cut through, and the population has grown to more than 16,000.

Still, in the quiet back streets of town, a hint of the past can be seen in stately homes well preserved.

I dedicate this book to Morristown and its people, to the town's historic past and its promising future, and to all those who have lived, worked, and played here from the time it was a quiet crossroads village until its bustling present.

Joan M. Williams
September 1995

One
People

A *c.* 1900 photograph of Macculloch Hall, the home of George P. Macculloch, who pioneered the Morris Canal. (MHHM)

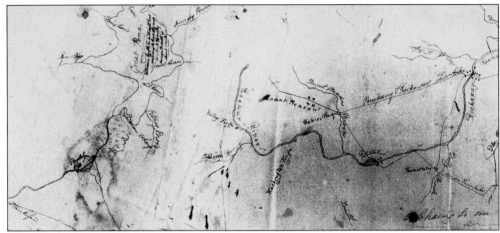

A c. 1820 sketch by George P. Macculloch of the Valley Forge and Dover, New Jersey, area as one of the preliminary plans for the canal. (MHHM)

Francis, Louisa, and Lindley Keasbey, descendants of George P. Macculloch, c. 1872. (MHHM)

Alice Lavinia Day, *c.* 1899. (MHHM)

Katherine Miller, at the piano, accompanies her daughter Dorothea (Dolly), while her other daughter, Charlotte, listens, *c.* 1900. (MHHM)

Dorothea Miller, great-granddaughter of George P. Macculloch, and James Otis Post on their wedding day in 1906. (MHHM)

Commodore Jacob Miller, grandson of George P. Macculloch, inscribed this *c.* 1900 photograph to his daughter Dorothea (Dolly). (MHHM)

Everett and Jack Post, descendants of George P. Macculloch, *c.* 1913. (MHHM)

The Macculloch family gathered for the birthday of Mary Louisa Miller, daughter of George P. Macculloch, in May 1878. The fanciful ship model was given by J. Pierpont Morgan, recognizing Jack Miller's service on the USS *Vandalia* during President U.S. Grant's world tour. (MHHM)

Alice Duer Miller and her infant, descendants of George P. Macculloch, *c*. 1901. (MHHM)

Probably the Macculloch family, in Macculloch Hall, *c*. 1878. (MHHM)

A c. 1915 photograph of W. Parsons Todd (at the wheel), with his stepmother, Emily, and his father, William Rogers Todd. W. Parsons Todd, who was affectionately known as "Mr. Morristown" because of his service to the community (which included two terms as mayor), restored Macculloch Hall. (MHHM)

Augustus and Mary Crane in the late 1880s. They bought Acorn Hall, now home of the Morris County Historical Society. (MCHS)

Mary and Augustus Crane sit on the lawn of Acorn Hall while their daughter Julia and her husband, Dr. J. Leonard Corning, stand on the porch, *c.* 1890. (MCHS)

The Loud children, probably Alexander Crombie, Henry Sherman Jr., Haroldene, and Marguerite, *c.* 1906. (MCHS)

Henry Sherman Loud Jr., *c.* 1900. (MCHS)

Unidentified ladies out for an afternoon drive, *c.* 1913. (MCHS)

Perry, the English coachman, with the Loud children, *c.* early 1900s. (MCHS)

A *c.* 1918 photograph of Dr. Alexander Crombie Humphreys, president of Stevens Institute of Technology from 1902 until his death in 1927. He had attended Stevens at night as an adult, graduating with high honors. His home, Lannock, was in Normandie Heights, Morristown. (MCHS)

The wedding of Marie Guillaudeu to H. Ten Broeck Runk at Lannock, the home of Dr. Humphreys. Dudley Guillaudeu gave his sister away. Bridal attendants were Evelyn and Edith Runk, Dorothy Carson, Mary Fish, and flower girl Marguerite Loud. Henry Abbott was best man, with ushers J. Dickinson Espe, Ruckman Lee, James Camby, and George Stephenson, c. 1910. (MCHS)

Thomas Nast's home on Macculloch Avenue, *c.* 1880. (Thomas Nast Collection, MHHM)

An 1885 image of Thomas Nast, who was famous for his political cartoons, particularly those lampooning the Tammany Hall organization in New York City, and his depictions of Santa Claus and Christmas. (Thomas Nast Collection, MHHM)

A signed photograph of Thomas Nast dated July 4, 1869. (J.M. Williams)

Thomas Nast (left, *c.* 1870) considered himself a twin in appearance to French artist Gustave Dore (right), whom he admired. (Thomas Nast Collection, MHHM)

Thomas Nast in costume, c. 1880. (Thomas Nast collection, MHHM)

Thomas Nast painting a self-caricature while on a lecture tour through the western United States, 1887. (Thomas Nast Collection, MHHM)

Thomas Nast painting a portrait of General Lee, *c.* 1902. (Thomas Nast collection, MHHM)

The Tammany Tiger, for which Thomas Nast was famous. (Thomas Nast Collection, MHHM)

A drawing by Thomas Nast urging contributions towards the pedestal on which the Statue of Liberty would be mounted. (Thomas Nast Collection, MHHM)

THE BARTHOLDI STATUE.

Even Liberty demands something substantial to stand upon.

One of Thomas Nast's drawings of Santa Claus. (Thomas Nast Collection, MHHM)

A Christmas cartoon by Thomas Nast. (Thomas Nast Collection, MHHM)

28

A Christmas cartoon by Thomas Nast, for which he used one of his sons as a model. (Thomas Nast Collection, MHHM)

Thomas Nast and his family on the steps of his home on Macculloch Avenue in 1884. (Thomas Nast Collection, MHHM)

William and Addie Watson on their wedding day, 1903. (JFPLMMT)

Sam Jenkins, a member of the Morristown High School Class of 1931, was considered one of their best football players. He later worked for the U.S. Post Office. (JFPLMMT)

Dr. Evelyn Lewis graduated from Morristown High School, c. 1919. After later graduating from Howard University, she became the house doctor at Provident Hospital, Baltimore, Maryland. (JFPLMMT)

A 1917 photograph of Alphas Watson, who served his country in World War I. (JFPLMMT)

Percy Steel (left), the first president of the Morris County Urban League, and Thomas Spruell, in the 1940s. (JFPLMMT)

32

The wedding of Madelyn Evans and David McAlpin at Twin Oaks. From left to right are: (front row) Marshall Mills, Ken McAlpin, Hugh Herndon, and Ted McAlpin; (second row) Ben McAlpin, Caroline Foster, David McAlpin, Madelyn Evans, and Gertrude Hall; (third row) Otto Mallory, William Vance, Fred Hahn, Clara Ogden, Gertrude Vernam (Forbes), Cornelia Willis (Vanderpool), Harriet Evans, Butler Duychinck, and Elsie Robinson; (standing at rear) Benjamin Franklin Evans and Harriet Bonbright Evans. Jason Billings can be seen in the background of this June 17, 1905 photograph. (JFPLMMT)

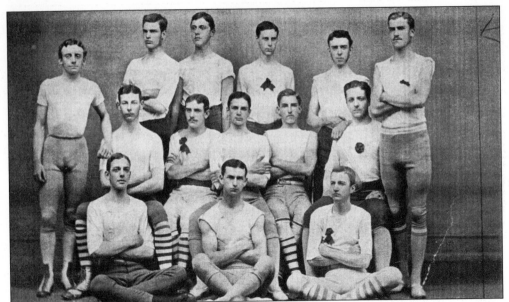

The Morristown Athletic Association in 1878. Shown are, in unknown order: Willard Walker Cutler, Mahlon Pitney III, Walter B. Wood, Theo. Ayers Jr., Carman Fitz-Randolph, Frederick Winston Merrell, Henry Spingler Von-Erden Davis, Paul Revere, Robert B. Merritt Jr., William Meeker Wood, Henry C. Pitney Jr., John O.H. Pitney, Thomas M. Fitz-Randolph, and Robert Wrightson Webb. (JFPLMMT)

The Dancing Circle at Morristown and Madison in July 1878. Pictured are, in unknown order: Henry S.F. Davis, Thomas M.F. Randolph, William Meeker Wood, Archibald Fitz-Herbert Maning, Edith M. Bartow, Charlotte Bartow, Caroline L. Hopkins, Alva Crocker, Walter B. Wood, Mahlon Pitney III, Henry C. Pitney Jr., Sadie L. Perry, Fannie L. Hopkins, Joseph R. Walker, Paul Revere, Lucy F. Randolph, Harry B. McCarroll, Minnie O. Condit, and Carman F. Randolph. (JFPLMMT)

Ready for a round of golf, *c*. 1913. (MCHS)

The Tennis Club poses at Olyphant Park, *c*. 1900. (JFPLMMT)

This 1918 photograph shows workers in the Women's Land Army taking a break. (JFPLMMT)

Alice Brewster in 1918 in the uniform of the New Jersey Division of the Women's Land Army. (JFPLMMT)

These members of the District Four Team were the Morristown baseball champions in 1922. From left to right are: (front row) Anthony Rich, Joseph Giordano, Andrew Nodoro, ? Machera, Anthony Bontempo, and Samuel Verrilli; (back row) Assistant Manager ? Kelly, Anthony Giordano, unknown, Russell Terreri, and Manager ? Farland. (JFPLMMT)

The Morristown Club celebrates its 25th anniversary on June 22, 1909. Shown are, in unknown order: Elbert Kip, Robert Foote, Leland Garretson, Joe Willis, Peter Frelinghuysen, Elbert Hyde, George Palmer, Henry Taylor, Noah Rogers, Ledyard Thompson, Livingston Roe, Ridley Watts, Ransom Thomas, Elmer Mills, William Shippen, George Dadmun, Dr. Granville White, John Brinley, Charles Chapman, and B.L. Chandler. (JFPLMMT)

A c. 1890 photograph of the Vail family at their homestead at the Speedwell Iron Works. Mary Lidgerwood, granddaughter of Stephen Vail (the Proprietor of the Works), is seated on the bench to the right. (Historic Speedwell)

Marion and Grace Douglas, c. 1890. (Jean and Homer Hill)

Two
Places

An 1837 painting of the Speedwell Ironworks. (MCHS)

Dickerson Tavern, where Benedict Arnold was court-martialled for irregularities while in command, c. 1900. (HSSH)

The Tempe Wick House. When Washington's troops were camped at Jockey Hollow during the terrible winter of 1779–80, Tempe hid her horse in her bedroom to keep it from scavenging soldiers. The horse's hoof prints are said to have been visible in the floor boards for many years. (June Kennedy, from a brochure published by the Water Company)

A *c.* 1910 photograph of the trolley tracks that were once laid in the dirt streets of Morristown. (JFPLMMT)

More trolley tracks, this time on Speedwell Avenue, *c.* 1910. (Neighborhood House)

The City Pharmacy, according to *Morristown and its Points of Interest, With Illustrations From Recent Photographs* (published in 1894), boasted the largest "soda water fountain" in the city. Mr. Headley, the book added, merited "fullest confidence" as a pharmacist. (Bernardsville Library Local History Room)

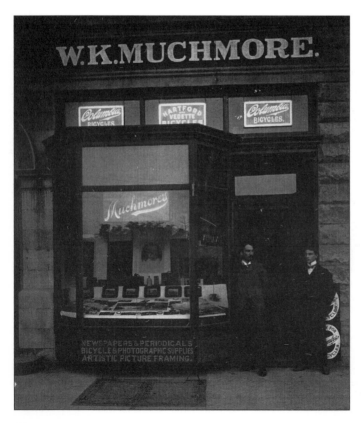

William Ketchel Muchmore and an unidentified man in front of Muchmore's store in 1900. Located on Speedwell Avenue, Muchmore sold newspapers and periodicals, bicycle and photographic supplies, and artistic picture framing. (JFPLMMT)

The Green, with Washington Street to the left and South Street to the right, c. 1912. (JFPLMMT)

James Fountain on the Green at the corner of Park Place and Speedwell Avenue, c. 1905. (THSSH)

The Green, *c.* 1900. (THSSH)

Park Place, *c.* 1910. (Jean and Homer Hill)

Park Place, looking west, *c.* 1900. (Bernardsville Library Local History Room)

South Street, with Market Street to the left, Park Place to the right, and Washington Street in the distance, *c.* 1910. (THSSH)

Mansion House, *c.* 1890. (MCHS)

Speedwell Avenue, *c.* 1930. (Neighborhood House)

Stores in the business district of Morristown, *c.* 1890. (JFPLMMT)

John Van Dorn and Lewis E. Applegit, employees, pose in front of the New York Cash Store in the early 1900s. (JFPLMMT)

A *c.* 1890 photograph of W.F. Day's establishment. Lined up in front are, from left to right: Edward Stanbrough, William Roy, Fred Baldwin, Wilbur F. Day (holding bicycle), Jeanette Mack Sucky, Georgie Kinsey, Maynard Day (sitting), Gus (a French chef), Charles Williams, Samuel James, Fred Day (sitting), Charles Pfeiffer, Harry Day, and Fred Krous. John Day and Mrs. Day watch from the windows above. It is said that William F. Day rode his bicycle to Washington in two days. Epstein's Department Store now occupies this site. (JFPLMMT)

The corner of South and DeHart Streets, *c.* 1890. (JFPLMMT)

The National Bank celebrates
its 200th anniversary, *c.* 1910.
(JFPLMMT)

A *c.* 1900 photograph of the First National Bank, located at the corner of Washington Street at
the Green. (JFPLMMT)

Epstein's Department Store has taken over the space (not to mention the merchandise!) of the Boots and Shoes and The People's Clothiers, shown here c. 1890. (JFPLMMT)

Bicycles were a common mode of transportation in the late 1800s and early 1900s. (JFPLMMT)

Standing on an unidentified corner in March 1889 are, from left to right: Peter Essex, Will Dustan, Andy Guerin, Henry M. Smith, Louis Umberham, and Mat Howe. (JFPLMMT)

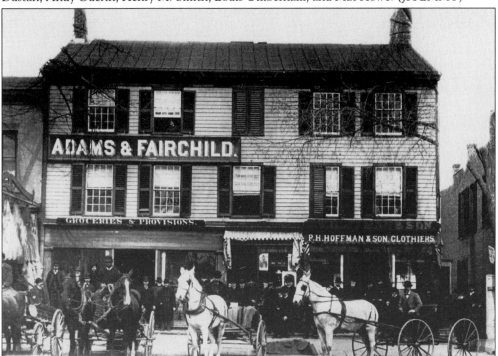

The former Arnold Tavern, where George Washington spent the winter of 1777–78, was, in 1886, Adams & Fairchild, grocers, and Hoffman Clothiers. The drivers of the carriages are Thomas J. Walker, ? Ammerman, and William Sowers. E.A. Van Fleet, H.H. Fairchild, and F.H. Fairchild are identified as standing behind on the left, with H.B. Hoffman, P.H. Hoffman, and Joseph R. Hoffman standing behind on the right in this 1886 photograph. (JFPLMMT)

The horse-drawn delivery vans of "Shelley Bros. Morristown Hygiene." William Shelley Sr. is the bearded gentlemen in the carriage. His son, William Jr., is standing on the roof in front of the window in this *c.* 1890 photograph. (MHHM)

Speedwell Avenue, *c.* 1913. (JFPLMMT)

Paul Babbitt is on the right in this 1906 photograph of an auto repair shop. Also shown are Ed Pullen, Carl Gluck, and Bill Jaggers. (JFPLMMT)

The Market Street Mission in August 1891. (JFPLMMT)

Police Headquarters. (MCHS)

A *c.* 1900 view of the formal garden of the Keasbey House, located next to Macculloch Hall on Miller Road. Anthony Keasbey married Edwina Miller, granddaughter of George P. Macculloch. (MHHM)

The old Presbyterian Manse on Morris Street after it became the first Morristown Memorial Hospital building in 1893. (JFPLMMT)

Memorial Hospital, probably on Madison Avenue. (MCHS)

Memorial Hospital, *c.* 1900. (Jean and Homer Hill)

A *c.* 1890 image of All Souls Hospital, which stood opposite the present building on Mt. Kemble Avenue until it burned down in 1918. (Bernardsville Library Local History Room)

All Souls Hospital, *c.* 1910. (THSSH)

Park Place in 1915. (MCHS)

A *c.* 1880 painting of Water Street and Speedwell Avenue by Edward Kranich. (MCHS)

A *c.* 1900 photograph of the Library and Lyceum, which housed a public reading room, the Morris Academy, and an audience hall and ballroom. (MCHS)

The Library and Lyceum burning on February 12, 1914. (JFPLMMT)

Armory, Morristown, N. J.

After the Library and Lyceum burned, the building became the armory for the Morristown Infantry Battalion, which was organized during World War I as a home guard. The armory is shown here *c*. 1917. (MCHS)

The new library on Miller Road in 1918. (JFPLMMT)

Patrons check out books in the new library, *c.* 1915. (JFPLMMT)

Washington Street in the early 1900s. (MCHS)

Washington's headquarters (the Jacob Ford Mansion), from an old woodcut. (Curtiss Collection, JFPLMMT)

The Civilian Conservation Corps working at the Ford Mansion in the 1930s. (National Park Service)

Washington's headquarters. Washington stayed in the Jacob Ford Mansion during the winter of 1779–80. (THSSH)

Madison Avenue, looking from Jefferson Avenue, c. 1890. (MCHS)

Maple Avenue, looking south, *c*. 1900. (Bernardsville Library Local History Room)

Madison Avenue, *c*. 1900. (Bernardsville Library Local History Room)

Madison Avenue and South Street, *c.* 1890. (MCHS)

South Street, looking from St. Peter's Church, *c.* 1900. (MCHS)

An October 1927 photograph of Ruth Higgins, who was born in the Schuyler-Hamilton House. She is shown here dressed as Betsy Schuyler when Betsy was courted by Alexander Hamilton. (JFPLMMT)

A view of the estate of Richard McCurdy. (MCHS)

The A.R. Whitney residence. (MCHS)

The Elms. (MCHS)

The Alcott residence. (MCHS)

The Van Vleck estate, *c.* 1920. (MCHS)

The Turnpike Inn, located on South Street. (MCHS)

County Club, Morristown, N. J.

The Country Club. (MCHS)

Lake Pocahontas. (THSSH)

A glimpse of Mills Ice Pond. (THSSH)

Edward Bunn, William C. Burnett, and James Armstrong ride in Lewis T. Bunn's "Aquatic Velocipede" on Lake Pocahontas, c. 1900. (JFPLMMT)

One of the few statues of Thomas Paine in the United States is located in Burnham Park. (Jean and Homer Hill)

The site of Fort Nonsense, erected during the Revolution. (MCHS)

Morris Street, c. 1950. (Jean and Homer Hill)

The Burnham Park pool was the site of this aquatic event, *c.* 1930. (JFPLMMT)

An early picture of the Park Theater on South Street. (JFPLMMT)

A group from Neighborhood House photographed *c*. 1900 when it was the Association of Work Among the Italians, which offered classes in English for the adults and day care for their children. (JFPLMMT)

A day care class at the Association of Work Among the Italians in 1913. (Neighborhood House)

In 1926 the Association, renamed Neighborhood House, began serving a multi-ethnic population. These two youngsters are shown in the 1950s. (Neighborhood House)

Neighborhood House children enjoy a parade in October 1948. (Neighborhood House)

MAYFIELD PRINTING

Boxer Frank Osborne receives an award from the first Afro-American executive director of Neighborhood House, Carmela Meade, and an unidentified businessman in 1953. (Neighborhood House)

Stephen Vail, owner of Speedwell Iron Works, in a c. 1840 image. (MCHS)

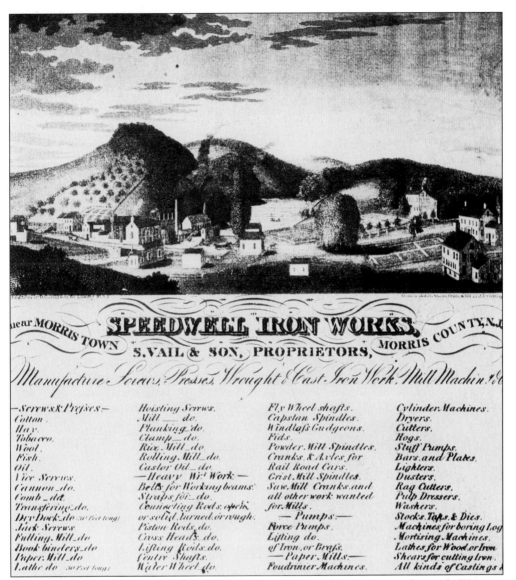

A *c.* 1800s billhead of Speedwell Iron Works, listing the products it manufactured. (Historic Speedwell)

Building where Morse invented the telegraph
MORRISTOWN, N.J.

The above photograph is of the building at Historic Speedwell where Samuel F.B. Morse, with the help of Alfred Vail, perfected his telegraph. (THSSH)

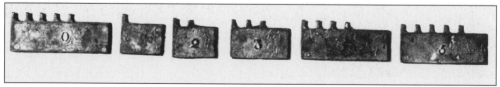

A sample of the original type, cast by Samuel F.B. Morse. (Historic Speedwell)

The dam at Speedwell Iron Works, showing the sawmill on the right, c. 1870. (Historic Speedwell)

Elm Street, near South Street, c. 1910. (THSSH)

L. C. Gillespie Residence, Picatinny Road.   MORRISTOWN, N. J.

The Louis Charles Gillespie estate. (MCHS)

This water tower was erected for Louis Charles Gillespie in 1894. It included a steam engine to pump water into a holding tank and a lookout on the top story. (MCHS)

Theodore Vail's private museum, now the Morristown Town Hall. (MCHS)

An 1898 bas relief portrait of Elizabeth Dodge by Mary B. Ryerson. (JFPLMMT)

The Morristown Post Office, *c.* 1920. (MCHS)

A *c.* 1930 photograph of the Morris County Court House, built in 1826. (June Kennedy, from a brochure published by the Water Company)

Three
Churches

The Green on a snowy day, with the old First Presbyterian Church and Soldier's Monument in the background, *c.* 1900. (THSSH)

The original First Presbyterian Church, painted by Miss Emma H. VanPelt, "according to some local tradition." (JFPLMMT)

The old First Presbyterian Church in 1870, with the Soldier's Monument in the foreground. (JFPLMMT)

The First Presbyterian Church at Park Place and Morris Street, *c.* 1910. (THSSH)

The Church of the Assumption on
Maple Avenue, *c.* 1900. (MCHS)

St. Peter's Church. (MCHS)

Church of the Redeemer, Morristown, N. J.

The Church of the Redeemer, *c.* 1900. (MCHS)

A *c.* 1873 photograph of the Methodist Church, showing the second church building (1841) on the left, as well as the third building (1870). (JFPLMMT)

The old parsonage of the Methodist Church, *c.* 1880. (JFPLMMT)

The Bethel A.M.E. Church, in a photograph taken early in this century. (JFPLMMT)

The First Baptist Church, located on Washington Street. (MCHS)

Four

Schools

A 1914 photograph of the Farmer's Hotel, said to be the site of the first public school in Morristown. (JFPLMMT)

The Mills Street School. (MCHS)

The Maple Avenue School, *c.* 1900. (MCHS)

Students of the Maple Avenue School gathered in the auditorium for a lecture in 1909. (JFPLMMT)

The Mt. Kemble School, c. 1890. Isaac Combs stands in the back row, second from left. (JFPLMMT)

Morris Academy students pose for a school picture, c. 1886. Frederick V. Pitney is second from the top left. (JFPLMMT)

Students at Miss Hazeltine's School, in a photograph taken during the summer of 1900. From left to right are: (front row) Elsie Nicoll (?), Mary Merrell, Vera Downing, unknown, and unknown; (middle row) K. Clarke, ? Cutler, Natalie Foote (?), and Bessie Cauldwell; (back row) Helen Downing, Allila Ewery (?), unknown, Miss Carrie Hazeltine, Matilda Frelinghuysen, Marguerite Veruary (?), and Josephine Flagg (?). (JFPLMMT)

Morris Academy in 1872, prior to its location in the Lyceum. (JFPLMMT)

The Morristown Select Classical School in June 1872 on the porch of the Pitney House on Maple Avenue. On the left side of porch are: (seated) Mahlon Pitney, Edward A. Muir, and Paul Revere; (standing) Nathan Bozeman, Augustus W. Bell Jr., George L. McAlpin, Harry B. McCarroll, Edward L. Hopkins, and Thomas M.F. Randolph; (standing in front of window) Alfred E. Decamp and Harry ?. In the center of the porch are: (seated in the front) Meyer L. Sire, Charles H. Davis, Benjamin Sire, D. Hunter McAlpin Jr., H.K. Toler (?), Albert I. Sire, Randolph McAlpin, William W. McAlpin, and Ingersoll Olmsted; (seated in the middle) F.W. Merrell and Alfred Elmer Mills; (seated on the top step) John O.H. Pitney, Principal George L. Wright, Assistant Wilbert Warren Perry, Theo. Ayers Jr., and John B. Ayers; (standing) Walter B. Wood, Sadie H. Pitney, H.C. Pitney Jr., James A. Webb Jr., Katharine Pitney, Mary Brayton Pitney, and Henry C. Pitney. On the right side of porch are: (seated in front of pillars) George L. Cobb and ? Myers; (seated in chair) Addison H. Hazeltine; (standing in front of pillars) William Meeker Wood; (seated in front of window) Looe (?) Baker. (JFPLMMT)

Miss Dana's School for Girls at South Street and Madison Avenue. (MCHS)

A 1900 photograph of Miss Dana's School. Miss Elizabeth Dana, a college graduate, opened her school in 1877. Her students received a collegiate curriculum including intellectual and moral philosophy, criticism and theology, history, chemistry, astronomy, reading, writing, and spelling. (JFPLMMT)

The students and staff of Miss Dana's School for Girls in 1900. (MHHM)

The Intermediate Class of Miss Dana's School in February 1903. From left to right are: (front row) Mary Smith, Aline Feuchtwanger (Brown), Louise Hastings, unknown, and Armande Ayers; (middle row) Florence Sittenham and Gladys Stults (Schenck); (back row) Madeleine Ayers (Thompson), Helen Humbert, and Betty Drinkwater. (JFPLMMT)

A 1916 photograph of Morristown High School students costumed for *Seven Keys to Baldpate*. Identified by last name only are: Peters, Lorter, LaMotto, Desson, unknown, Jones, Penn, Eldeyt(?), Sanderson, Reinhart, Williams, Mosle, and unknown. (JFPLMMT)

The Morristown High School graduating class of 1919. From left to right are: (front row) Margery ?, Bessie Erwin, unknown, Maud Byram, Marian Moody, Anna Day, Louise Bockoven, Sarah Bohm, Dolly Pierson, Emily Eager, Emily Rood, unknown, and Marie Broderick; (second row) unknown, unknown, Gertrude Hoffman, Ruth Peer, Helen Eichlin, Clara Beckwith, Frances Luby, Ruth Udall, Pauline Udall, Lillian McHarrie, Corelia Pierson, Madeliene English, Elizabeth Holley, Mae Sutton, and unknown; (third row) unknown, unknown, Beatrice Kline, Marjorie Coursen, Frances Napp, J. Burton Wiley, Clara E. Brown, Ray Cecil Carter, ? Duffy, Evelyn Lewis, Frances McConnell, Mildred Sheerin, Virginia Dickinson, and Harold Karn; (back row) Edward Marinaro, Roland Clark, unknown, unknown, John Gannon, ? Gaty, ? Young, J. Parker, Courtlandt Parker, Harry Davis, Logan Grupelli, ? Gaty, James Whitehead, Griffith Vaughan, unknown, John Reed, unknown, Frank Sanson, Howard Black, Albert Michelfelder, Lewis Thompson, and Roland Chamberlain. (JFPLMMT)

Motto: Nitere ut praestes

Class Song

Alas! the days have now sped by
    Which we have held most dear.
We leave past joys with many a sigh
    As our parting hour draws near.

Chorus—
Then give three cheers for naughty eight
    Hurray, hurray, hurray.
We all will give while we shall live
    Three cheers for red and gray.

Let's e'er remember naughty eight
    And the joy it does recall.
The Crescent, symbol of our fate
    Will be cherished by us all.

To M. H. S. our praise we bring
    With loyal hearts and true.
We'll all unite to shout and sing
    Long life, dear school, to you.

Commencement Exercises
of
Morristown High School

Edith Wenman
Marjorie Phillips *Laura Schmarudorf*
Margaret Murphy *Clara Woodhull*
Lulu Garrabrant *Marion Douglass*
Mildred Arrowsmith *Will Baker*
Maude Welsh *James Roberts*
Isabel Slater *Carl Sturgis*
June 26, 1908 *Howard Garrabrant*
Ethel Davis *Boyd Berry*
Katherine Lane *Fred Wilke*
Gaynell Combs *Chas. Van Ness*

A graduation program for the June 26, 1908 graduation at Morristown High School. (Jean and Homer Hill)

Program

The American Navy	Wm. C. Baker
Read by Katherine A. Lane	
Some Friends from Our Bookshelves	Marjorie M. Phillips
Music The Miller's Wooing	Faning
Chorus	
The Preservation of our Forests	Marion L. Douglass
Presentation of Diplomas	
Music "In the harbor we've been sheltered" Arranged	
from the Opera Martha	Veazie
Chorus	

Program

Music Gloria in Excelsis	From Farmer's Mass
Chorus	
Prayer	
Airship Development	Frederick H. Wilke
Music The Voyagers	Facer, arranged
Chorus	
Old Time Schools and School Books	Marion Isabel Slater
Read by Mildred Arrowsmith	
Music The Old Guard	Paul Rodney
Chorus	

The Ladies Seminary, *c.* 1900. (MCHS)

The Morristown School For Boys, now the Morristown-Beard School, *c.* 1895. (MCHS)

Five
Wheels and Rails

The first station of the Morris and Essex Railroad at Maple Avenue and DeHart Street, c. 1840. (JFPLMMT)

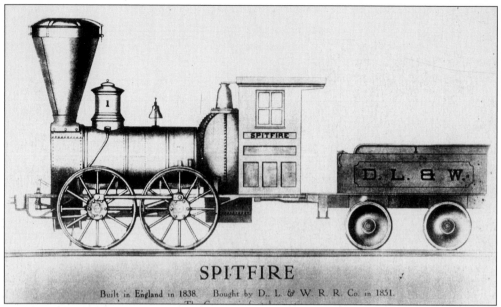

SPITFIRE

Built in England in 1838. Bought by D., L. & W. R. R. Co. in 1851.

Purchased in 1851 by the Delaware, Lackawanna and Western Railroad, the Spitfire, built in England in 1838, was the D.L. & W.'s first locomotive. (JFPLMMT)

A steam engine at the Morristown railroad station in 1895. The building was red brick with a slate roof. (JFPLMMT)

The coal dock at the Pruden and Burke Coal Company. Included in the group of men are Grandpa Pruden and Edward Wesley. (Jean and Homer Hill)

An early ticket from the Morristown and Erie Railroad.
(Jean and Homer Hill)

Horses and buggies wait at the Morristown station for passengers from the steam engine, *c.* 1900. (THSSH)

The circus train unloads, *c*. 1900. (JFPLMMT)

This railroad wreck occurred near Evergreen Avenue, *c.* 1910. (JFPLMMT)

The first electric train glided into Morristown station on September 22, 1930. (JFPLMMT)

The eastbound Phoebe Snow at Morristown station, *c.* 1950. (Jean and Homer Hill)

Lackawanna R. R. Station,
Morristown, N. J.

The present Morristown station, *c.* 1920. (Jean and Homer Hill)

In this *c.* 1915 photograph the trolley to the left, with its pole down, apparently waits for the other trolley to clear the junction. (JFPLMMT)

The first trolley car rumbled into Morristown on August 27, 1909. (THSSH)

A motor delivery van in front of Fitzpatrick Ford, *c.* 1916.

The repair truck for the New York and New Jersey Telephone Company, shown here in 1890, was pulled by a horse. (JFPLMMT)

The short-lived Morristown-Madison Auto Bus Company operated from July 20, 1912, until January 31, 1914. (JFPLMMT)

Six
Community Helpers

Visiting Nurses ready for their rounds, *c.* 1914. (JFPLMMT)

An early telephone operator. (JFPLMMT)

In August 1888 a committee was appointed for the celebration of the 25th anniversary of the Independent Hose Company No. 1, including a dinner held in the Schmidt building on South Street. From left to right are: (front row) J. Frank Lindsley and Henry M. Smith; (middle row) Harrie T. Hull, Heyward G. Emmell, and George L. Muchmore; (back row) D. Farrand Sturges, Dr. Joseph R. Hoffman, and Eugene Carrell. (JFPLMMT)

SPEEDWELL FIRE COMPANY.

MORRIS COUNTY, STATE OF NEW-JERSEY, ss.

This is to Certify, that *Albert Kumbherville* was regularly admitted a member of this Company on the *fourteenth* day of *April* eighteen hundred and *twenty eight* agreeably to the provisions of an act of the Legislature of this state, passed the fourteenth day of December, eighteen hundred and twenty-six.

Dated at Morris-Town, the *14"* day of *April*, eighteen hundred and *twenty eight*

J M Kerr Foreman.

J Ogden Canfield Secretary.

This certificate admitted Albert ? as a member of the Speedwell Fire Company in April 1828. The company was organized August 13, 1827. (JFPLMMT)

A c. 1890 photograph of members of the Independent Hose Company No. 1. From left to right are: (seated) Harrie T. Hull and Heyward G. Emmell; (standing) J. Frank Lindsley, James R. Voorhees, Charles A. Covert, Henry M. Smith, and Dr. Joseph R. Hoffman. (JFPLMMT)

This *c.* 1890 photograph of a chemical engine is labeled "Hose Co., and Chemical Engine Co.— 'Independent Hose.'" (JFPLMMT)

Chief F.A. Trowbridge reins in Tom and Jerry on the Resolute Hook and Ladder truck, *c.* 1900. (JFPLMMT)

The elaborate reception room of
the Independent Hose Company,
c. 1890. (JFPLMMT)

Policemen at the old station house
on Speedwell Avenue, *c.* 1890.
(JFPLMMT)

The Independent Hose Company, *c*. 1888. Included in the photograph are: Augs. W. Bell, D.H. Rodney, Charles H. Dalrymple, W.N. Corriell, F.E. Babitt, H.G. Wolff, Eugene Carrell, Dr. A.A. Lewis, J.F. Runyon, Charles H. Green (former member), G.E. Voorhees Jr., D.F. Sturges, J.F. Lindsley, J.R. Voorhees, H.B. Hoffman, J.B. Stevens, Frank Schuremand (former member), James T. Clark (former member), James McGuinnis, L.F. Sturges, Theo. Ayres, H.M. Smith, H.T. Hull, C.W. Ennis, C.S. Bird, George C. Smith, W.H. Becker, I.R. Pierson (former member), Dr. C. Dobbins, H.A. Bray, Dr. Joseph R. Hoffman, George V. Muchmore, H.G. Emmel, and E. Van Fleet. (JFPLMMT)

Morristown letter carriers, *c.* 1900. From left to right are: (front row) William Beach, Ed Hutchings, and Dick Headley; (back row) Joseph Pierson, Joseph Ambrose, George DeGroot, and William Taylor. (JFPLMMT)

The Home Guard at the Morristown Armory, *c.* 1917. (JFPLMMT)

Officers of the Morristown Infantry Battalion in 1917. Major Gillespie is seated in the center of the first row. (JFPLMMT)

Seven
Events

The Buffalo Bill parade during a show on Speedwell Avenue in June 1898. (JFPLMMT)

An early broadside, including the program of a concert noted in the center of the sheet. (June Kennedy)

A 1906 broadside from the South Street Presbyterian Church. (JFPLMMT)

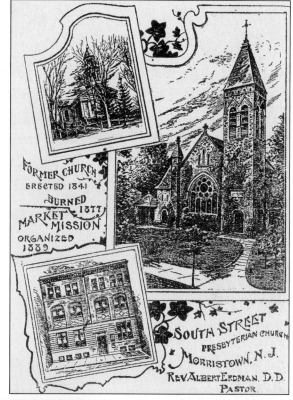

The Speedwell Merchant's Association poses before their "annual outing," c. 1930. (Neighborhood House)

Women campaigning for the vote in 1915. Mrs. Henry John Gregory is among them. (JFPLMMT)

Local women gathered to campaign for the vote in October 1915. (JFPLMMT)

Some men didn't seem to think too well of women voting. This photograph was taken in 1915. (JFPLMMT)

Families and friends give Battery F a patriotic send-off in 1917. (JFPLMMT)

The 1917 Memorial Day Parade photographed as it moved along Speedwell Avenue. (JFPLMMT)

The Fairchild Drum Corps makes its last public appearance, for the dedication of the Fort Nonsense Monument on April 27, 1888. Marching are L.P. Hannes, H.H. Fairchild, Lemel E. Fairchild, Clifford A. Fairchild, and F.H. Fairchild (bass drum). William Beers carried the colors. Also shown are H.W. Miller, H.O. Marsh, A.H. Venisor (?), W. Vanderpool, G.G. Kip, J.A. Webb, F. Nishwitz, J. Thatcher, Reverend A.M. Sherman (?), J.E. Taylor, and C.T. Werts. (JFPLMMT)

Nurses on parade, possibly on Memorial Day, *c.* 1918. (JFPLMMT)

The statue of George Washington opposite the Ford Mansion is unveiled, *c.* 1930. Miss Mabel Clarke, the donator of the statue, is second from the right. Dr. Henry Nehemiah Dodge, third from right, gave the land. Also in the group are Mayor Potts and the sculptor, Mr. Roth. (JFPLMMT)

Morris County celebrated its 200th anniversary with a parade on October 12, 1939. (Archie Beiser)

Marchers parade around the Green for Morris County's anniversary celebration on October 12, 1939. (Archie Beiser)

This *c.* 1930s photograph, taken in front of the Cenotaph, includes: Mayor Clyde Potts; Margaret Wilsey; American Legion National Commander Paul V. McNutt; State Commander Herbert Blizzard; Post 59 Commander Joseph B. DeGroot; State Chaplain Reverend Gill Robb Wilson; State Adjutant Roland Cowan; Elmer P. King; Horace C. Jeffers; Harry C. Mitshall; Leon Cone; Louis Dempsey; Robert McNeil; Anson J. Beckwith; Max Husselrath; and Lester Block. (JFPLMMT)